It Is Always NOW!

MARDI LONG

Archway Publishing books may be ordered through booksellers or by contacting:

Archway Publishing
1663 Liberty Drive
Bloomington, IN 47403
www.archwaypublishing.com
844-669-3957

ISBN: 978-1-6657-0944-6 (sc)
ISBN: 978-1-6657-0943-9 (e)

Library of Congress Control Number: 2021914062

Print information available on the last page.

Archway Publishing rev. date: 07/30/2021

Many thanks to the numerous people who have inspired and encouraged me throughout my life. Each one has added grains of inspiration that have added up to what I hold dear today. I am sure I could not name them all. Sometimes it is just a fleeting comment that can cause us to look at something in a new way.

Special thanks as well to those who helped me in the early stages of my "little book." Some of the feedback may have seemed trivial at first glance. But in the end, I realize that every observation helped me shape my message. Call me grateful.

❧

"God does nothing prematurely,
but, foreseeing the end from
the beginning, waits till all
is ripe for the execution of
His purpose!" [1]

CONTENTS

INTRODUCTION

Dear Fellow Traveler,

Is it just me, or is our digital world the very epitome of information overload? How do we sort through the constant and often conflicting information that rushes at us every day? I have found it to be so much easier with a solid, personal belief system in place. This little book is based on my personal journey that began anew in 2002 and continues to evolve as it always must. It is fueled by my determination to constantly validate and expand that personal belief system.

It is not the goal of my little book to tell others how this all works. Everyone must realize their own journey. Rather, it is my hope that the reader might find some insights, encouragement, and awaken curiosity!

Mardi

FREE WILL

"Is it possible that GOD created mankind because His love nature needed creatures on which to lavish His love?" [2]

It is my conclusion that "free will" is the foundation of GOD's universe.

He does not want robots - He wants sentient beings who come to Him and His love of their own - yes - "free will." The latch to the door of our heart is on the inside - only we can open it - GOD will never force His way in.

THE KINGDOM OF GOD

The Kingdom of GOD is here and now – as much as is humanly possible in this life. All GOD asks of us is that we love one another. Just as He loves us.

Sounds so simple! And yet we fail over and over in our attempts to truly love. Not to worry – GOD is always there when we fail and when we ask for that help. He never gives up on us and we must never give up trying.

MARK 9:24
JOHN 10:10

THE PATH TO DISCOVERY

It is important to approach these steps in the right order! Each step builds on the one before. Focus on GOD through the constant power of His love.

This journey is always a work-in-progress! It evolves throughout our lifetime. We cannot do it alone!

1. Open the Door of your heart - Claim the JOY GOD offers to all.

2. Seek - Focus on the TRUTH - Receive GOD's LOVE [love in].

3. Find the DEEPER TRUTHS - Persevere and Grow - Welcome GOD's PEACE as your TRUST in Him evolves.

4. Reinvent and transform - Follow new pathways – Embrace the HOPE that endures.

5. Do not judge others - To do this you must truly LOVE them [love out]. Have FAITH that GOD alone is the judge.

6. Set no limits - Experience RAPTURE.

1. OPEN THE DOOR!

Let the Sunshine In!

One day it dawned on me:
It all has to start with JOY!
Not giddy, human joy - no, no, no!

The JOY that can only be found when you open up your heart's door to let the SUNSHINE of GOD's love in!

This changes everything!
This makes everything else possible!

JOY: A calm luminosity inside of you that lets you savor and interpret the life around you. As you open the doors of your heart and mind, this feeling can become the food for your passion!

PSALM 89:15
PHILIPPIANS 4:6-7

When you are angry or depressed or anxious you freeze up - right? You tend to shut the world out. You do not - cannot - enjoy or embrace the life around you. Some days you may not "feel" the Joy. Or you may get there for a brief moment and then it is snatched away by the relentlessness of life.

Keep reaching for it. When you do have true Joy, you wake up in the morning fresh and eager to embrace that new day!

RELAX, GROW & GLOW

2. SEEK AND FOCUS

Never Stop Seeking the Truth!

Create an environment where GOD's love can reach you.

Having a set time and place to study will increase your chance of success.

Stay focused - yes, read and study - the Bible and other books that inspire you!

What is curiosity? Webster: "desire to know and interest that leads to inquiry." AKA: Something that keeps nagging you in the back of your mind. Most things that make us curious do not have simple answers. Very little in life is black and white. That is why we must constantly keep our hearts and minds open.

MATTHEW 6:6
MATTHEW 7:7

Slowly, you will put more things into perspective and learn to open your heart and mind to new possibilities. It is then that you are likely to discover ever deepening satisfaction, excitement, and even contentment.

So many things that you never knew were even possible!

YOUR SECRET GARDEN

3. FIND AND GROW

Meditate Day and Night

Do not rush it - let it happen one step at a time:

One tiny "byte"/insight at a time.

Ponder each morsel to more fully absorb it.

GOD is not in a hurry and you must not be!

Follow the insights you find as you study.

Paul speaks of "milk" and "meat" as it relates to our level of understanding. First, we learn the basic truths (milk) that must always remain our foundation. As we grow and dig into the deeper truths (meat), we will begin to grasp and internalize the intricacies.

PSALM 19:1-6
ROMANS 11:33

Do you ever look up in the sky at night and wonder what is up there?

I mean, there is this never-ending universe - right? Sometimes the thoughts are all jumbled together. Some use a journal to gather their thoughts. I prefer typing on my computer.

But whatever works for you....

WONDER WISELY

4. NEW PATHWAYS

Let God's Love Reinvent You

Only the presence of GOD in our hearts and minds can truly change us:

Yes, REINVENT a new us!

We know that our brain has pathways, and that we can create new ones over time with consistent effort.

Do not be surprised or become discouraged when you falter or even fail miserably! Just keep on - keeping on.

VISUALIZE what you know GOD intends for you to be and to do! Use each "failure" as an opportunity to learn and grow. Then forget about it and move on.

ISAIAH 42:16
COLOSSIANS 1:13
ROMANS 12:2

Our lives are made up of many experiences: Some good – others not so much. Each experience is like a tiny mosaic tile. All of the tiles add up over time to define who we are. As we let the Joy in and build new pathways, damaged and mismatched tiles are replaced with beautiful ones. God can take all of our mistakes and brokenness and guide us as we slowly become the person we were created to be.

BE NOT AFRAID

5. LOVE! JUDGE NOT!

Have Faith - God Is the Judge

GOD is the judge because only He can see the heart and soul. GOD has this - He does not need our help!!

Yes, we are each responsible for judging ourselves and striving to follow what we learn as we learn it.

Our job - our only job - in relating to others is to take time to listen and let friendship evolve and above all - JUST LOVE THEM!

What Francis of Assisi said: "Preach the gospel every day - If necessary, use words..." [3]

I SAMUEL 16:7
LUKE 6:37
ROMANS 13:8

Relationships are like flowers. They need care and feeding to keep them alive and growing. Look for each opportunity to show that you care. Then, listen for each opportunity to share what you know. But never get the two confused. Make sure that the ground is well prepared by love before you attempt to plant any seeds.

PHONE A FRIEND!

6. TRANSCEND!

Seek Heavenly Realms

We can have our "Mount of Transfiguration" moments:

YES - in this life!

Why are we so afraid of Meditation? The Bible speaks of it often.

This is really what it comes down to: We must consciously clear our minds and hearts of all that blocks the presence of GOD - of all that hinders us – of all that holds us back - of all that makes us afraid.

"This world deserveth nothing but the outer court of our soul!" Samuel Rutherford [4]

PSALM 39:3
PSALM 63:6
MATTHEW 17:1-7

Slowly, as we obtain peace of mind and heart - our Joy becomes full. When we can truly believe, we will obtain the presence of GOD's love. Then we will be able to rise above all that is here and now. You can't make this up. You can't force it. Keep your eyes on our Lord and let it come to you. When you least expect.

SET NO LIMITS!

ASSURED OF SALVATION?

Yes, I really believe that this is what the Bible teaches.

It has come to my attention that many of the parables provide answers:
- The Lost Coin: We must keep seeking!
- The Lost Sheep: The Shepherd is always there to bring us back to the fold.
- The Talents & Sown Seeds: If we do not tend to our faith, it will wither & die.
- The Bad Manager and Feast: As long as we keep trying, the blood of Jesus will cover our failings with His cloak of mercy.

KEEP IT SIMPLE!

Plug into the Joy – New each morning!

Open your heart! Yes, it is that simple! Let the Sunshine in – God will guide and inspire you. Open the door!

Each day is NOW. Each moment is NOW. There is never a wrong time to embrace and refocus and get up and keep on going. "NOW is the time." It is always the time.

IT IS ALWAYS NOW!

Do not look back. Do not look down. Just onward and upward with eyes on JESUS.

What is it about stained glass?

Why - It is the light shining through!

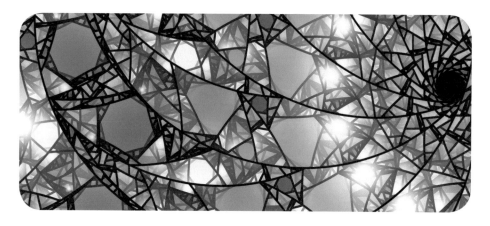

If we let GOD's love in - that love and light can shine through us for all to see!

II SAMUEL 23:4
LUKE 11:36
MATTHEW 5:14

WHEN IN DOUBT - PRAY!

Dear GOD, You know I want to believe. But right now, I am just not feeling a connection. This is me opening the door to my heart. Please flood me with the Joy of Your love. Show me You are there. I will follow You. Amen

THEN: Do not try to force anything to happen. Pray, read GOD's word, and live your life. GOD will do the heavy lifting.

Perhaps it is now time to reconnect with GOD in a different way. Just wait and follow - He will lead.

"**Wait** for the Lord; be strong and take
heart and **wait** for the Lord."
Psalm 27:14 [5]

YOUR PERSONAL JOURNEY

BibleGateway.com can be a very useful tool. You can look up texts from different versions of the Bible in multiple languages. You might also find that comparing verses in various versions can be enlightening. Sometimes just one different word can spark a new insight. You can search by exact passage or a string of words. They also provide other tools that you may find useful. For example, you can get a Bible verse sent to your email each morning.

There are many other books you will not want to leave out. Books can inspire you and enhance your understanding as you grow. Search on Amazon or other internet sites or even go to Barnes and Noble or your local Christian bookstore. Holding a book and turning the pages still has an appeal.

Start tracking your own journey. That is the only one that really matters for you. You can accumulate quotes from your study and Bible verses that especially speak to you. I use MS PowerPoint because it facilitates my visual view of looking at life. You might like MS Word. Or a handwritten journal. Whatever works for you:

Wonder Wisely and Enjoy Your Journey!

IN CONCLUSION

Back to the introduction. How does one's personal belief system help in sorting through the information overload? It is very subtle and will vary with each individual. I admit that I struggle to put words to it. But I feel that in all fairness to my readers, I must try.

As you study and pray, your conclusions will slowly evolve and solidify. Then, as you encounter new ideas and concepts, you have something to compare these against. In some cases, you may dismiss this information. In other cases, you will find that this new idea, this new concept fits into your belief system and adds strength and meaning to it.

The important thing is to never completely dismiss a new idea or concept at first glance. But, also do not accept it at face value without careful consideration. Almost always there is some "truth" in it. Evaluate all new information carefully. That is what it means to "wonder wisely."

REFERENCES:

[1] Jamison, Fausset, Brown's Commentary on the Whole Bible, 2971, Zondervan, New Ed edition (February 1, 1999) Location 87849

[2] WWJD, Nick Harrison, Perfect Bound, Page 81

[3] WWJD, Nick Harrison, Perfect Bound, Page 3

[4] WWJD, Nick Harrison, Perfect Bound, Page 49

[5] Holy Bible, New International Version®, NIV® Copyright ©1973, 1978, 1984, 2011 by Biblica, Inc.® Used by permission. All rights reserved worldwide.

NOTES

NOTES

VISIT OUR WEBSITE:

Here you will find information about other books that are available.

MardiLong.com

Printed in the United States
by Baker & Taylor Publisher Services